cascade

trout
pool

rfles

kingfishers
nesting

fallen
log

KA-BOOM!

My life begins when gray-bellied clouds
fling down rain that seeps underground
filling crevices in soil and stone

until...

out I spill
from a spring
in the heart of the forest.

TRILLIUMS

YELLOW
WARBLERS

A shallow creek or mossy brook,
I'm small and easy to overlook.

WHAT ARE HEADWATER STREAMS?

The smallest of flowing waters,
headwater streams are where
rivers are born.
Some flow all year,
others only when fed
by rain or snowmelt.

RED EFT

But I am a **headwater stream**—
the secret source of rivers.

My waters work wonders
by turning one thing into another...

MINK

LOOK UNDER ANY ROCK.
Healthy streams are great habitats
for juvenile aquatic insects.

LOUISIANA WATERTHRUSH

When trees shed leaves
I fix a feast
for insect nymphs and larvae.

They shred and nibble,
graze and grow,
turning old leaves
into new life.

SCRAPERS
gnaw algae off rocks.

SHREDDERS
nibble the leaves.

MAYFLY
NYMPH

STONEFLY NYMPH

STREAMS RECYCLE LEAVES.

Microscopic fungi
and bacteria grow
on sunken leaves,
turning them into
slimy snacks for
juvenile insects such as
stonefly nymphs and
caddisfly larvae.

BROOK
TROUT

COLLECTORS

filter out crumbs.

BLACKFLY LARVAE

Together,
they keep small streams
clean and become food
for larger predators.

CADDISFLY LARVA WITH A
CASE OF PLANT MATERIAL

Caddis worms build clever homes
and hide inside among my stones,
safe from hungry fish.

Some use pebbles and grit.
Others gather scraps of plants.

Each kind makes its own design
and binds it with sticky silk.

ADULT
CADDISFLY

A CASE FOR A CADDIS

Caddisfly larvae, or **caddis worms**,
build portable homes called cases to hide
themselves, protect their soft bodies from
predators, and weigh themselves down
against strong currents.

CADDISFLY LARVAE WITH
CASES OF PEBBLES

WHEEEEE! Now my current whirls and races over rough and rocky places. Welcome to my RIFFLES!

In these burbling, bubbly spots larvae cling beneath the rocks, waiting to snag a snack.

HANG ON!
Stonefly and **mayfly nymphs** have tiny claws for clinging.

MAYFLY NYMPH

STONEFLY NYMPH

A **blackfly larva** deposits a bed of silk on a rock and anchors itself with more than 100 tiny hooks on its bulbous behind.

But they must hold on tight
or I might wash them
awaaaay . . . .

UNDERWATER HURRICANE

Riffles are turbulent
places where streams
rush over rocks,
delivering food and
oxygen to aquatic
insects clinging to
stones and gravel.

DAMSELFLY
NYMPH

WHOOSH!

Down I tumble
over a jumble
of boulders.

SPLOOSH

. . . right into a pool,
where fins flicker in the gloom.

Which larvae will meet their doom?
Watch out—here comes a trout!

BROOK TROUT

CATCHING THE DRIFT

Insect nymphs and larvae that lose their grip or let go to feed may get washed downstream as **drift**. They make an easy meal for trout lurking in the pools below **cascades** (miniature waterfalls) and riffles.

Watching trout swirl in schools,
Kingfisher hunts my quiet pools.

Waiting. Hovering.
Diving—

SPLASH!

Young trout dart behind rocks.

SONGBIRDS
feast on clouds of insects
emerging from streams.

STEEP BANKS
and dense thickets provide
safe places for birds to nest.

FLASH!

But Kingfisher rises
with a silver prize
and gulps it down,
my water sparkling
in that feathery
crown.

BELTED KINGFISHERS
nab prey from the water.

Mayfiies and their
aquatic kin
leave my waters
and shed their skin.

Why?
It's time to FLY!

ADULT
MAYFLY

A DAY WITH WINGS

After living underwater for months,
aquatic insects **metamorphose**
into winged adults. Adult mayflies
don't have mouths because they
don't eat. Most live only a day or
so—just long enough to mate and
lay eggs in the water.

EMERGING ADULT

They spread their wings,
flit, spin, dip back down
to lay eggs in my shimmering shallows.

MAYFLIES

EBONY JEWELWING DAMSELFLY

SPLASH!

Who's this frolicking in my waters?
Sleek, slippery river otters!

They play and chase, then dive below
to hunt crayfish and minnows.

SEEING UNDERWATER

Transparent inner eyelids help otters
spot underwater prey. They can hold
their breath for up to eight minutes!

RIVER OTTERS

RIVER OTTERS
live on land but hunt in clean
streams, rivers, ponds, and estuaries.

CRAYFISH

FRESHWATER MUSSELS

WHUMP!

A wall of branches halts my flow.
I slow and rise, I flood and grow . . .
into a POND!

NORTH AMERICAN
BEAVER

ENGINEERS OF THE STREAM

Beavers gnaw down saplings and branches
to dam streams, creating ponds around their
dome-shaped lodges. A lodge's underwater
entrances keep out coyotes and other predators,
while the inside living spaces stay high and dry.

PAINTED
TURTLE

Beaver dams
are thick and strong,
but nothing holds
me back for long.

Seeping, dripping, leaking,
trickling, I find a way
and then flow on.

MALE WOOD
DUCK

BEAVER LODGE

A HOME FOR ANIMALS

Beaver ponds provide habitat for
aquatic insects, amphibians, reptiles,
fish, wild ducks, and other creatures.

Dark clouds tower.

KA-BOOM!

A thundershower!
Filling with rain,
I roil and churn,
gouging and scouring my banks.

I'd wash them away if not for the trees
gripping my shores with sturdy roots.

FILTERS OF THE RIPARIAN ZONE

Roots of trees and plants
hold streambanks in place and filter out
pollutants that may wash down from roads
and parking lots during storms.

STREAMS NEED TREES

Streamside trees shade the water, keeping it cool and healthy, and autumn leaves fill streams with food for aquatic insects!

Through the moonlit
woods I flow,
past turtles, owls,
a thirsty doe.

HAVENS FOR WILDLIFE

Many animals use the banks of streams and rivers as highways,
watering holes, and rest stops on their travels and migrations.

TWO-LINED
SALAMANDER

Creatures seek me night and day,
some to drink, some to rest.
Some come to hunt,
some to nest.
Some dwell beside
me all their lives.

BARRED OWL

Born of rain,
I swirl and change
around each bend,
joining others of my kind
as I flow to the lowlands.

GREAT BLUE
HERON

Now I grow wider, deeper, darker,
and I know with a sudden shiver,
that I am no longer one small stream—
I've become a magnificent river!

Author's Note: Headwater Streams

Even mighty rivers like the Mississippi and the Amazon begin as headwater streams. Flowing downhill, they join other streams, merging into tributaries and eventually into great rivers flowing to the sea.

As a girl growing up in Maine, I loved exploring a brook that flowed past my house not far from the vernal pool that inspired my first book, *The Secret Pool*. I spent hours at the brook watching water striders skitter across the surface, turning over rocks to search for two-lined salamanders, and spying on streamside birds and painted turtles. I always wondered where the brook began and where it was going. I never found its source, but I discovered that it flowed into the Mousam River at the end of my street. I still like to stick my feet in that brook's cool water in the shade of birch and hemlock trees.

A brook or stream is a kind of **ecosystem**—a community of organisms that interact with their environment and one another. Healthy streams teem with animal life, especially **macroinvertebrates**—creatures without backbones, such as mussels, snails, crayfish, and young aquatic insects. Rich in insect life, clean, cool, tree-shaded streams also host fish such as trout and provide habitat for birds, mammals, reptiles, and amphibians.

Streams turn old leaves into new life through the magic of **food chains**, which link to form **food webs**. Life in and along streams, as in other ecosystems, starts with plants, which make their own food from sunlight. When leaves fall into streams in autumn, they are colonized by microscopic **decomposers** such as fungi and bacteria. These rotting leaves are eaten by herbivorous aquatic insects such as mayfly nymphs. Trout and other fish eat the insects. Small trout, in turn, are eaten by kingfishers. This is just one example of the many food chains in a stream, which connect to form a food web.

If one link in a food chain is broken—for example, if pollution kills aquatic insect larvae—the effects ripple through the food web. The fish that eat the insects go hungry and disappear, and then so do kingfishers, herons, and other fish eaters. This is one reason it's important to protect small streams.

Headwater streams and the rivers they form also provide drinking water to millions of people around the world. The next time you gulp a glass of water, remember that it probably started flowing to your well or public water supply from a headwater stream many miles away.

I hope this book inspires you to explore your nearby streams, discover who lives there, and help protect these special places.

The Cast of Characters

Here are a few of the creatures you might see or find signs of in or beside a healthy stream.

AMPHIBIANS

Red efts are juvenile (young) red-spotted **newts**. Their red-orange skin warns predators such as raccoons and bullfrogs that they're poisonous! Red-spotted newts have a fascinating lifecycle. After hatching from eggs in the water, they live as aquatic larvae for a couple of months and then undergo a **metamorphosis**, swap-

ping gills for lungs and turning into bright-red efts, which are terrestrial. After two to four years of life on land, eating grubs and small insects, red efts grow gills again, mature into adult red-spotted newts, and return to the water for the rest of their days.

BIRDS

Barred owls are famous for their call, "who-cooks-for-you, who-cooks-for-you all?" They live in forests, often near water, where they hunt for rodents such as mice and squirrels, as well as birds, amphibians, reptiles, and invertebrates. They will also wade in shallow water to catch crayfish and fish! Barred owls nest in tree cavities 20 to 40 feet above the ground. The ranges of these homebodies are often as small as one square mile.

Belted kingfishers hunt from bare branches and other perches over streams, rivers, ponds, and bays. When this bird sees a fish or crayfish, it dives headfirst into the water with its eyes closed and nabs its prey with its bill. One way to find a kingfisher is to listen for its rattling call as it dives or hovers over the water searching for prey. Kingfishers excavate nest burrows in sandy banks. Unlike most birds, the female belted kingfisher is more colorful than the male, with a rust-colored band that gives the bird its name.

Great blue herons stalk frogs, fish, reptiles, invertebrates, and rodents in marshes and the shallows of rivers, ponds, and bays. The largest heron in North America, this bird wades slowly or stands perfectly still and then strikes, spearing or snapping up prey in its long, powerful bill. Great blue herons nest in colonies of up to several hundred pairs, building large nests of sticks in trees, bushes, and even on the ground.

Louisiana waterthrushes feed and nest along clean, fast headwater streams. These chubby, sparrow-sized birds teeter in the shallows as they forage for aquatic insects such as caddisfly larvae. Waterthrushes are not thrushes at all, but a kind of small songbird called a warbler. They breed in the eastern US and migrate to wintering grounds as far away as northwestern South America.

Wood ducks nest in tree cavities over or near ponds, streams, and swamps. Ducklings hatch with a full coat of fluffy down. They leave the nest only a day after hatching—jumping out of the

entrance and tumbling as much as fifty feet to plop into the water or onto the ground without getting hurt! If they immediately find their way to water. Wood ducks will also use nest boxes to raise their families.

Yellow warblers sing "sweet, sweet, I'm so sweet" from willow thickets along streams and brushy edges of wetlands. The males have rusty streaks on their necks. These small, brilliant birds can be seen in every state except Hawaii during migration or breeding season. Like most songbirds, they eat insects and caterpillars, which they also feed to their young, helping to keep destructive pests in check.

FISH

Brook trout live only in clean, cold streams, rivers, and lakes. They are dark olive green with yellow and red squiggles and spots, and white edges on their ventral (belly) fins. These carnivores eat tadpoles, insects, salamanders, minnows, small water snakes, and crayfish. They are eaten by herons, ospreys, kingfishers, and larger fish. Brook trout spawn in the fall. The female fans her tail to make a shallow nest, or redd, and lays up to 400 eggs. After the male fertilizes the eggs, the female covers them with gravel. The eggs incubate over the winter and hatch the following spring.

INSECTS AND OTHER INVERTEBRATES

Blackflies bite humans and other mammals, but their larvae help clean streams. Shaped like squat bowling pins and anchored to rocks underwater, they filter out bacteria, algae, and plant debris from fast-flowing streams with feathery appendages on their heads. After a blackfly larva pupates, the adult floats to the surface on a bubble and flies into the air.

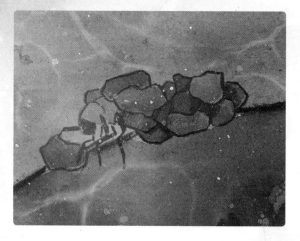

Like mosquitoes, only female blackflies bite—looking for a blood meal in order to lay her eggs!

Most species of **caddisfly** larvae, or caddis worms, build cases from pebbles and sand or plant material to protect and camouflage themselves from predators such as brook trout and waterthrushes. They bind these materials together with their special silk, which is like stretchy, double-sided tape that stays sticky in water. They also use these cases like cocoons, sealing themselves inside to finishing growing and eventually emerging as adults that resemble moths with narrow wings.

Crayfish are small freshwater relatives of lobsters. As they prowl about on the bottoms of clean streams and ponds hunting small invertebrates and feeding on detritus, they also have to keep an eye out for predators. Crayfish are a favorite food of many animals, including trout, raccoons, herons, and humans, especially in the southern US, where they're often called crawfish or crawdads.

Damselflies, such as the ebony jewelwing, are related to **dragonflies**, but there's an easy way to tell them apart. When at rest, a damselfly holds its two sets of wings parallel to its body, while a resting dragonfly's wings stick out perpendicular to its body like an airplane. Damselfly and dragonfly nymphs (called **naiads**) and adults prey on other insects. Naiads can sling their jaws forward and snap up unsuspecting prey, including small fish. One adult dragonfly can eat several hundred mosquitoes in a day!

Freshwater mussels are important stream cleaners that filter out algae, bacteria, and pollution. Some of the 500 or so species of freshwater mussels have amazing strategies for spreading their young throughout a stream. For example, the Ouachita kidneyshell mussel releases larvae in jelly-like capsules that resemble small fish. When larger fish bite the capsules, they burst, releasing larvae that stick to the fish's gills, growing into tiny mussels that eventually drop off and settle on stream bottoms.

Adults of most **mayfly** species don't have mouths—their lives are so short they don't need to eat! Mayflies live only a day or two as adults, just long enough to mate and lay eggs in streams and ponds. Like dragonflies, damselflies, and many other aquatic insects, they spend most of their lives—up to two years—as nymphs feeding on the bottoms of streams and ponds. Most mayfly nymphs are herbivores, but some eat **detritus** (rotting plant and animal matter), and a few are carnivorous. Nymph and adult mayflies are eaten by trout and other fish, and birds feed on adult mayflies.

Stonefly nymphs always have two antenna-like tails, or cerci, while mayfly nymphs usually (but not always) have three. The best way to tell stonefly and mayfly nymphs apart is to look at their feet through a magnifying glass. Stonefly nymphs have two claws on each foot, while mayfly nymphs have one. Like mayflies, adult stoneflies often lack functioning mouthparts and live only a day or two. These insects inhabit only clean streams—their disappearance from a stream indicates declining water quality.

MAMMALS

Beavers can't resist the sound of running water. It has been shown to make them build and repair dams! The largest rodents in North America, beavers are a **keystone species**, which means that many other animals depend on them. The ponds created when beavers dam streams pro-

vide habitat for insects, amphibians, reptiles, fish, birds, and other mammals. While beavers are sometimes considered a nuisance, beaver ponds have been shown to improve stream quality, making life better for all animals—including humans.

Deer are surprisingly picky eaters and choose the most nutritious plants they can find in every season. The riparian zones along healthy streams provide a banquet of flowering plants, grasses, ferns, shrubs, and trees for these herbivores, who must eat up to eight percent of their body weight every day—12 pounds of leaves and plants for a 150-pound deer! Deer also drink from streams and use riparian zones as travel corridors and places to rest.

Millions of **humans** depend on headwater streams for drinking water. Unlike other animals, humans can harm streams by allowing pollution to flow into them, using too much water for agriculture and other purposes, and destroying riparian zones by cutting down trees. Humans can, however, work together to restore and protect wild streams.

River otters are excellent swimmers who can hold their breath underwater for more than four minutes as they hunt for prey such as small fish, crayfish, and freshwater mussels. Active at dawn and dusk, they are difficult to find, but you can sometimes spot signs of their activity. Look for otter slides, shallow trails about eight inches wide in grass, mud, or snow where these playful animals slide on their bellies into the water. River otters often use the same places for their "latrines"—look for small scat (poop) flecked with fish scales and crushed shells.

REPTILES

Painted turtles bask on logs and streambanks during the day and snooze in shallow water in the evening. They hunt underwater for snails, crayfish, and aquatic insects, poking their heads

into vegetation to frighten their prey out of hiding. In the winter, these cold-blooded creatures hibernate in mud at the bottoms of ponds. Their hearts slow down, and they stop breathing until spring sunshine melts the pond's roof of ice.

Two-lined salamanders live under rocks along the edges of streams. These skinny yellow amphibians with a pair of dark racing stripes down their backs hunt for aquatic insects and other prey while trying to avoid being eaten by owls, raccoons, and trout. Female two-lined salamanders lay their eggs on the bottom surfaces of submerged stones and logs and protect them from predators.

More About Streams and How to Protect Them

BOOKS

Trout Are Made of Trees, by April Pulley Sayre, illustrated by Kate Endle, Penguin Random House, 2008

Water Is Water: A Book About the Water Cycle, by Miranda Paul, illustrated by Jason Chin, Roaring Brook Press, 2015

WEBSITES

American Rivers: Rivers of the U.S.
https://www.americanrivers.org/rivers/discover-your-river/us-rivers/

Discover Water
https://www.discoverwater.org/investigate-freshwater/

EPA How's My Waterway
https://mywaterway.epa.gov/

EPA Watershed Academy offers links to educational resources and activities for grades K-12.
https://www.epa.gov/watershedacademy/grade-k-through-12-watershed-learning-links

World Wildlife Federation's Freshwater: Our Most Important Resource
https://explore.panda.org/freshwater

Glossary

algae (singular, **alga**): A large group of plants, many of them tiny, with no true leaves, stems, or roots. Most grow in water. In streams, algae look like green scum covering rocks or floating in the current.

aquatic: Living in water.

bacteria (singular, **bacterium**): Microscopic, single-celled organisms that are able to eat and rapidly multiply. More bacteria live on Earth than any other living thing. Some cause disease, but most help digest food and break down waste into chemicals and nutrients.

camouflage: Coloration patterns that help an animal blend into its surroundings.

drift: Aquatic insects and other organisms that are swept downstream by current.

fungi: Mold, mushrooms, and other organisms that feed on decaying matter.

habitat: The place where a plant, animal, or other organism lives.

invertebrate: An animal without a backbone, such as an insect.

juvenile: A young animal.

larva (plural, **larvae**): The newly hatched form of an amphibian or invertebrate, such as a tadpole or a caterpillar.

metamorphosis: The process by which some organisms, such as insects and amphibians, grow into adults.

molt: To shed an outer covering such as skin, a shell, or feathers.

nymph: A juvenile aquatic insect that grows into an adult by molting.

organism: A living being.

pupa (plural, **pupae**): A stage of insect growth in which a larva develops into an adult inside a cocoon or other case.

riffles: Places where streams rush over rocks, mixing oxygen into the water.

riparian zone: The land along a stream or river.

Tilbury House Publishers
Thomaston, Maine
www.tilburyhouse.com

Designed by Frame25 Productions
Printed in Canada

Kimberly Ridley is a science writer and children's book author living on the coast of Maine. Her picture books *The Secret Pool* (Tilbury House, 2013) and *The Secret Bay* (Tilbury House, 2015) have earned multiple awards, including two Riverby Awards for Outstanding Natural History Books for Young People from the John Burroughs Association. *The Secret Stream* is Kim's third guided tour of the wetland habitats that are critical to life on Earth. See more at kimberlyridley.org.

Megan Elizabeth Baratta is a children's book illustrator living in central New York with her husband and two cats. She loves rendering scenes of ordinary life and showing their quiet beauty, as in her picture book *Most Days* (Tilbury House, 2021). Her illustrations for *I Begin with Spring: The Life and Seasons of Henry David Thoreau* (Tilbury House, 2022) were praised as "glorious" in a starred review from *School Library Journal*. Visit her at barattastudio.com.

beaver dam

otters playing

wildflower field